Sally Jenkinson was born
has been writing and pe
more than a decade, and
internationally in Sweden

C000184725

Her work has recently been featured in The Morning Star,
Lighthouse Journal, Emerge Lit Journal, The #MeToo
Anthology from Fairacre Press, and on BBC Radio 4's 'Power
Lines'.

She is a care worker and community arts producer, and is
currently working towards her MA in Creative Writing from the
University of Gloucestershire.

She has lived in Sheffield, Bristol, and Brighton, and now lives
in the Forest of Dean with her cats, husband, and various
fierce and magical children.

Pantomime Horse, Russian Doll, Egg

Sally Jenkinson

Burning Eye

BurningEyeBooks
Never Knowingly
Mainstream

This edition published by Burning Eye Books 2022

www.burningeye.co.uk

@burningeyebooks

Burning Eye Books
15 West Hill, Portishead, BS20 6LG

ISBN 978-1-913958-31-2

For Polly Jean Reader
and Jackie Wilson
and Jean Brown
and Poll Bidmead
and on and on.

Contents

Author's Note

Ultimately, these poems are about the magic of labour and birth. But my birth experience wasn't totally straightforward, and these poems explore the whole experience. They also carry the weight of my historic hospital trauma.

What I mean to say is, if you are preparing to give birth for the first time, maybe don't read them now. They'll still be here waiting for you on the other side, when you're tucked up in clean sheets with a cup of tea.

Also, I want to acknowledge that birthing is not the only way of entering motherhood. Plenty of mums do not give birth. Indeed, I did not give birth to some of the children I have had the honour of parenting. Mums who didn't give birth – I see you and I love you.

Similarly, I want to acknowledge that not all people who give birth are mums. Surrogates, trans and nonbinary parents – I see you and I love you.

Pantomime Horse

The latent phase

You may feel irregular contractions. It can take hours, or even days.

At a poetry reading, when someone pauses for too long mid-poem, sometimes the audience tentatively start to clap, thinking this is their moment. I am on the edge of my seat, peering at the open mouth of a poet. My hands are held apart in mid-air. Should I applaud the end of the first act? So far we have been one character, secretly played by two actors. Pantomime horse. Russian doll. Egg.

First stage

Stay upright and gently active. Help your baby move down into your pelvis.

A walk in the woods. June has been busy, exploding the forest into life. I tell Sam I'm still not really sure this is it. He tells me I have been pausing every eight minutes to howl into the trees' sun-speckled clerestory. I watch *Monster-in-Law*, starring Jennifer Lopez and Jane Fonda. Eat nachos. Say prayers. In the bath, Elvis asks me to take his hand and his whole life too.

Second stage

You may want to sit, stand, lie on your side, kneel or squat.

Cycling through a paddy field in Vietnam, I saw a giant water buffalo wallowing on her side in the mud. Pasting herself in protection from the high noon sun. She writhed and huffed and squirmed in a way that was hard to distinguish as

11

pleasure or pain. There was no way I could help her, even if she was stuck. Where else could she go? No other water or shelter for miles around.

Third stage

This way lowers the risk of heavy bleeding, but increases the chances of you being sick.

The compulsion to take photographs of animal dung, footprints, eggshells on the forest floor. I had wanted to watch the placenta appear, study the process. But time is not linear. Coulomb's law. I was busy holding the whole universe together. Careless of me – to lose an organ, and not notice it leave. Later, they gave it to my stepdad in a plastic bag. We buried it at Deepdean. It's yours now.

Then

It's a good idea to have the baby lifted on to you straight after they are born.

Flotsam and jetsam. Sink and swim. Ebb and flow. Sleeping and waking. Waking. If she dies, I'll die. Carefully pat yourself dry. Stitches will usually dissolve. Lovesick. After the gold rush. Pee three times, click your heels together and you can all go home. Open water. The open road. I can't. Something is wrong. I can't stand it. I can't stand. The moon is rippling and it won't keep still.

Nymphaea

We set the birth pool by the books,
hoping this line of poets might –
Atwood to Vuong – share by some osmosis
a little of their ecstasy and grace.

I've always loved the lowering down
to water, but never more than tonight.
Your rabbit heart, fast-thumping in the wings –
waiting for your cue to find your light.

I call you softly down, my little moon.
The stage is set, the lake holds us like lilies
as we begin to swim across to shore.
I task myself with love, with making space –

I thought that I would start to feel like *open*,
but actually it feels a lot like *bloom*.

Birth Plan

I hope to do this at home
because hospitals are choked with ghosts.
Trip hazards, fragments of bone,

memory loss.

Hospital Transfer

It seemed to start out so well, but somewhere
along the way, I was picking a scab
or peeling the label on an old bottle or pulling out hair

or perhaps the frayed edge of an old cleaning rag
and suddenly the whole thing unravelled.
I had hoped to finish the whole job in the pool. I had

hoped for a gold star. I play for time, treadle
the machine of myself, pretend to be working.
If I get out of the pool, I will disintegrate. I muddle

an excuse; the kitchen floor is lava. I am hoarding
atoms and flotsam. I am beached. She insists.
My baby and I are two trapped snakes, crawling

tail in mouth. Midwife – stuck vowels and terse lips.
I am not doing it right. I am failing.
I was such a good girl before. The gymnastics

of effacement. The performance of dilating.
I put my hand between my legs and found
an unstable star. I have lost my way. *Fake it*

till you make it. We might not. The morning sound
of beeps and clicks and the sliding whistle of the blackbird
is my baby singing to me. So profound

for one so young. *Mama, haven't you heard?*
It's time to ask for help. It's time to ask for help. It's time
to go. Fingers paint the pain in broad, blurred

shapes. Across the wide Severn, the hospital cries
out to me, *I didn't mean to lose him I'm sorry*
come back and I'll be better let me try.

Of course, nothing matters but her new-grown body
(slick floors / sharp corners / lost love / the abyss).
Here comes our redemption arc, sure and sturdy.

No bone-old fears can compare to this.
My portly chauffeur arrives through the fog; he
ushers and shuffles, a sweet conformist.

Wagons roll! calls my paramedic, cheerfully.
        I am splitting like an apple in the hands of a farmer.
Wagons roll.

Still Life with Second-Hand Birth Pool

Inflatable bath squats the floor.
Still water, pinked with my brute self.
Purple ball where I retched and keened.
Stone walls stand a foot thick, unfazed.

Old towels across the room where
we opened and opened. Where I
touched her head, where I thought I could
but I couldn't. Quick red footprints
out into the daylight, wounded tracks
submitting to the bright unknown.

In Which I Walk on Water, or Am Water, or I'm Drowning

scooping up buckets of myself
so I don't pour
down the side of the hospital bed

so high and narrow
and me
all liquid

should be in a wide shallow dish
something with a lipped edge
to stop me from spreading

have always known we are
sixty percent water and yet

it is shocking how much pours out
when the levee breaks

bones deliquesced
blood thinned or spilling
flesh itself a kind of vapour

lost through transpiration
and hanging damp in the air

I drink myself
as the baby drinks all the amniotic fluid daily
what am I
if not a column of water

a nurse tries to hold down my arms
but I'm wet everywhere
like an octopus

I slither from her grasp and luge away
in search of somewhere safe

wet slaps of my loose limbs
on the floors and walls as I climb

salty waves outside
lurching at the windows
any second now the storm
will breach this cabin
and I won't know myself from the sea

hairline crack in the pane
becomes a scurry of drips
and then
        there she blows

                        sewn up in the snake pit

               hull is unsupported
               hogging and sagging

      a rub of the green
           saltash luck

marrying the gunner's daughter

                            I eat the anchor

the thing about water is
you either swim or you don't

End-of-the-Pier

for Sam

How interesting to suddenly accept that I am dying /
How interesting that pleasure piers so often burn down /
Suspicious circumstances / Bitter flames meeting salt water
/ Driftwood charring on the briny surface / Steel beams
buckling coyly with the strain / I push with the flat soles of my
feet against something solid / Use my hands to force away
the water above me / For the final time / Heart open for the
knowledge / Before I go I have to ask / *What was this all for?*

I have always been off-season / Windswept and bawdy, holy
and sad / Paint-peeling glamour and wood rot / Here is my
jazz-hands finish / I'm so sorry, my love / I could not pull off
this final trick / My head crests the water's surface / A last
gasp like the first sip of whisky after a long night on stage.

My chest is pitched and sodden against his chest / His arms
wrapped sturdy around me / My breath is his breath / He has
been there the whole time / Holding on / And as my body
comes apart in his hands / I know this / I was loved / I was
loved / I was loved.

Perimineralisation

I cast your great-grandad's ashes overboard.
A sea burial.
He crossed the bar
and yet he is Morse code in our blood.

Your father makes things out of wood.
He is so quiet
I never know what he's thinking.

His granddad, who I never met,
was a Quaker too.
We wait in silent expectation of the light.

Your grandma cared for a man
who walked across Europe as a boy
escaping a war.

I don't know
how I'm going to explain
this world to you.

Your dad climbs trees.
When he reaches the crown
he can breathe.

My grandma always gives me clothes
three sizes too small.
She remembers women shrinking.

Your uncle died.
I still can't talk about it.
Sometimes I hear him calling my name
across the hallway.

Your dad always knows when we need ritual
and when we need air
but he doesn't like holidays.

Your great-great-grandma gave me a house.
She banged on the table at parties.   She bred boxers.
Her armchairs were covered in lace.

Some of your family are aquatic fae,
fish out of water,
clutches of eggs or archetypes.

Others are flightless ratites,
home birds
and mute chordates.

I can't keep track of the
holy stones I'm offering.
I can't remember if any of this is true.

You were a keen twist in my heartwood
and now you are a red giant.

I am carbonising myself
to arrive at you.

Found (In My Birth Notes) Poem

Name of proposed procedure or course of treatment
include brief explanation if medical term not clear
(Trial of instrumental delivery and/or caesarean section)
Statement of patient
MS of patient
something of patient
410 205 7870 date of patient
Mum patient
Please read this form carefully

*I am leaning over the back of a gurney, keening with the low
thrum of a slow-turning earth.*

If your treatment has been planned in advance, you should
already have your own copy of page 2, which describes the
benefits and risks of the proposed treatment.

*His mouth moves. I only hear the whispering of the mycelium
beneath us.*

If not, you will be offered a copy now. If you have any further
questions, do ask – we are here to help you. You have the right
to change your mind at any time, including after you have
signed this form.

I sign the form with the power of my mind.

*(It turns out I actually did sign it with a pen. I'm looking at my
signature right now. Not bad penmanship for an intermediate
mass in a late phase of stellar evolution).*

statement of health professional (to be filled in by health
professional with appropriate knowledge of proposed
procedure, as specified in consent policy) I have explained the
procedure to the patient.

In particular, I have explained: the intended benefits

The baby, here safely. Also, for this to be fucking over.

I agree to the procedure or course of treatment described
on this form. I understand that I will have the opportunity to
discuss the details of anaesthesia with an anaesthetist before
the procedure, unless the urgency of my situation
prevents this frequently occurring risks ... I –

*It is 1905. Mary Ann Bidmead, née Harris (known to her loved
ones as Poll), goes into labour without any idea how the baby
will come out. Fourteen children pass through her body in her
lifetime.*

understand that any procedure in addition to those described
on this form will only be carried out if it is necessary to
save my life or to prevent serious harm to my health. extra
procedures that may become necessary during the procedure:
(repairing injury/tear
hysterectomy)

*One of those babies is born already carrying in her body the
ovum that will become my mum.*

(please specify) I have been told about significant and/or
foreseeable additional procedures that may become necessary
during my treatment .... I have received the following
information The following written information has been
provided
signature (PRINT) .... Date

We mummers, Galoshins, brave amateur actors –
playing the parts of each other,
Pace Egging through time and space,
sleeper agents inside one another's blood.

The proposed procedure may involve: general and/or regional
anaesthesia but this might change/and further consultation
with an   anaesthetist.   Local   anaesthesia

The manner in which doctors intervene is clumsy;
          who can blame them?
Appearing awkwardly at the door, like a house guest
interrupting a blazing row.
Nevertheless I am grateful
          for their safety net.

For their asking   if they can come in and rummage around,
          trying not to slip over in the mess,
stepping in   when we've no more ideas for how the baby
will come out,
pulling life from life from life.

Forensics

1999   a boy-man lifts me onto a chest freezer
full of ice pops and Zooms
pushes my knees apart he smells of Wrigley's (blue)
and B&H (blue)
and WKD (blue)
he says everyone thinks I'm weird

I see him outside a pub in my hometown
twenty years later the day I find out I'm pregnant
and say hello politely

2009   a man I love has a text affair
with a woman I admire
he tells me it means nothing
he tells me he is on medication for his brain
which means he can't get hard
for anyone but me

good-bad
kryptonite
my cunt can kill or cure

2019   a man stands between my stirruped ankles
asking calmly if I am sure if I am happy
for him to cut

yesyesyes I say
I would have given an arm
given him my beating heart
to get my daughter here safely

he sews me up tighter than before
I didn't ask him to

How to Birth a Great Big Baby

Strip lights   thinned to bright slits

Legs   gone now

Voice   whisked away

Doctors   aliens

Husband   satellite

Insides   out

Myself   tethered by a long ribbon   spacewalking

Stainless steel   stasis

Gown   unsound

Polyurethane   skin

Salt spray   grasping

Gutsy   hope

Exploded view   to make space for landing

Stand back please

         she needs   so   much   space

Golden Shovel for My Baby and Me

after Neil Diamond

Splayed under bright lights, I hand myself over, then
I am only a portal. Only an exit. I
wanted to be active. Pious, feral and alone. I saw
a woman on the internet do this just with low sweet moans; her
baby's first sight was not the stern face
of a doctor. I am deadened from the waist down and now
they are slicing and cleaving and I'm
the meat. I push and push but I'm just the butcher's table. Just a

mum.   Heretic, convert, devotee, believer.
You unfold, all tentacles. My darling octopus, you are not
the enemy. I forgot what I was doing this for. We are a
balloon rising up and up. All eyes trace
our ascent into the big blue everything. You are made of
me, but now you are yourself. You are the absence of doubt.
Slicked with life, a soft heap on my chest. Definite. We are in
the familiar part of the movie. The crowd goes wild. My
body derelict, the theatre dissolves. Neither of us seems to mind.

Piss Twice Before You Can Go Home

two healthcare assistants come with me to the toilet
I am mute with pain   no small talk

perched
on the cliff-edge of consciousness
try my best to piss

I can't go home until

a sound escapes from my mouth
            iron filings and grit-salt
            prayer
            the centre cannot hold

one of them
starts laughing audibly behind her hand
we don't acknowledge it

my shame is filthy, slicked with sweat
I shove it quickly in my dressing-gown pocket
where it squats for almost a year

I can hear my daughter crying

once
I saw a wild boar at the roadside
split open   red
hit by a speeding car
and its legs were still trying to make it stand up

nobody could stop to help it
the road was too busy and fast
the traffic just kept coming and coming

After All That I Can't Remember a Single Lullaby, So I Sing That Song From *Oliver!*

consider yourself part of the furniture
the NCT lady said newborns can crawl
whatever we've got, we share
I daren't loosen my arms in case you slip

the NCT lady said newborns will crawl
along Mum's landscape to the first latch
but I daren't loosen my arms in case
you slip awkwardly, I lower you across my chest

along this landscape to the first latch
you are my first daughter, but also my third
awkwardly I lower you across my chest and hope
every shred of light, every shaky step forwards

you are my first daughter, but also my third
we don't have a lot to spare
every shred of light, every shaky step forwards
consider yourself
                    home

The Goddess Myth

When she falls asleep on my chest I feel as though I could levitate

I'm scared to go home because my body is old music

My atoms are vibrating with love

A lady who had twins went home before me

I can hear the trees talking to each other a mile away

My first bowel movement is still almost a week away

We are stitched backwards through time to the ancients who created us

My dear friends left me voice notes

I am going to be good enough for you

I can't listen to them without crying

I am going to hold the lid on the saucepan

Generous emptiness. I can't think about my stitches

Your tiny hands, your tiny ears, your tiny wail

I won't write a poem for another year

You're the best thing I've ever made

One day you'll ask me a question I can't answer

I can't wait to show you the forest

Please God, let me get this right

The miracle of your voice   How you keep breathing and
breathing

The honour
          of watching you make yourself.

Acknowledgements

'Golden Shovel for My Baby and Me' originally appeared on the series *Power Lines* on BBC Radio 4, in August 2021.

'Pantomime Horse' originally appeared in issue 20 of *Emerge Literary Journal*, in September 2021.

'Piss Twice Before You Can Go Home' originally appeared in issue 23 of *Lighthouse Journal*, in February 2022.

Thank you so much to Bridget and Clive at Burning Eye for all your support, hard work and alchemy.

Thank you so much to Becca Lewis for the cover artwork, and Camilla Adams for the cover design. I'm so grateful for your talents.

Thank you to Dr Angela France for your expert editing advice.

Thank you to Devotion Sunday School for providing space and catalyst for me to write some of these pieces.

Thank you to Lesleyanne Martin for being a great mum to your two, and showing me what that looks like. I really miss you.

Thank you for your continued support, inspiration and love as I figured out how to write this: Hannah Ayin, Holly Blackwell, Laurie Bolger, Rosy Carrick, Olive Carrick, Lucy Ellis-Howell, Nise Hinds, Nuala Honan, Mick, Sarah, Sadie and Eve Jenkinson, Becca Lewis, Lizi Morse, the NCT angels (Amreen, Annabelle, Claire, Lorna, Sarah and Sophie), Polly Jean Reader and Sam Reader, Hannah Reader, Jenny Reader, Deanna Rodger, Fran Webb, Jackie, Martyn and Elliott Wilson.

Lightning Source UK Ltd.
Milton Keynes UK
UKHW021316020922
408223UK00006B/505

9 781913 958312